A CROWELL HOLIDAY BOOK

EASTER

BY AILEEN FISHER

Illustrated by Ati Forberg

Thomas Y. Crowell Company   New York

CROWELL HOLIDAY BOOKS
Edited by Susan Bartlett Weber

NEW YEAR'S DAY
LINCOLN'S BIRTHDAY
ST. VALENTINE'S DAY
WASHINGTON'S BIRTHDAY
PURIM
ST. PATRICK'S DAY
PASSOVER
EASTER
ARBOR DAY
MAY DAY
MOTHER'S DAY
FLAG DAY
THE FOURTH OF JULY
LABOR DAY
THE JEWISH NEW YEAR
COLUMBUS DAY
UNITED NATIONS DAY
HALLOWEEN
ELECTION DAY
THANKSGIVING DAY
HUMAN RIGHTS DAY
HANUKKAH
CHRISTMAS
THE JEWISH SABBATH
SKIP AROUND THE YEAR

Easter is a time of rejoicing.

It comes in spring, a joyful time for everyone. The cold dark days of winter are over. Birds return to sing. Grass and flowers begin to make a new carpet for the earth.

The date of Easter is not the same from year to year. But it always comes on the first Sunday after the first full moon in spring.

For Christians Easter Sunday is the greatest religious holiday of the year. It is a day of joy. It celebrates the Resurrection of Jesus of Nazareth, who rose from death to new life many years ago.

Long before the celebration of Easter, people celebrated a spring festival. They feasted and sang. They danced and gave gifts. They rejoiced over the rebirth of life in the fields and woodlands.

After the Resurrection, the Christian religion spread to many lands. The joy of the Resurrection became mingled with the joy of the spring festival. Both celebrations stood for new life. Both stood for new hope in the hearts of men.

And so it is not strange that many of the customs of the old spring festival became part of our celebration of Easter.

The Easter egg is a good example of a custom that began many thousands of years ago.

For ancient peoples, the symbol of new life was an egg. When the shell broke, new life came into the world. In India and Egypt, people thought that the world itself began as one huge egg. Then the world-egg split in two. The upper half became the heavens, and the lower half the earth.

For countless years it was the custom to give eggs as gifts during the spring festival. The ancient Persians and Chinese did it. So did the people of northern Europe during the Middle Ages. So do we today.

Usually we do not spend a great deal of time decorating our Easter eggs. We have fun dyeing them in bright colors and putting on simple designs.

But in some countries of Europe decorating eggs has been a great art for many years.

In Poland and Yugoslavia girls and women paint fancy designs on eggs before they are dyed. They paint the designs with beeswax, and try to make each one a little different. Flowers stand for love, a deer for good health, the sun for good luck, a rooster for wishes that will come true.

After the design is finished, the women dip the eggs in bright red dye. The design under the beeswax stays the natural color of the egg.

In Russia, in the old days, artists made beautiful eggs of crystal and gold. Sometimes they decorated them with jewels for the Czar and his family. One goldsmith won worldwide fame for the jeweled Easter eggs he made.

Many of the Easter eggs of Europe have crosses on them and other religious symbols. They carry words or letters that mean CHRIST IS RISEN. This is a common greeting on Easter Day.

People keep these beautiful gift eggs for years and years, and display them at Easter time.

The Germans were the first to make an Easter-egg tree. Carefully they pricked a hole at each end of the shell and blew out

the inside of the egg. Then they colored and decorated the shells and hung them on a tree or bush outdoors.

Sometimes they used bright ribbons and tinsel and other decorations on an egg tree indoors.

German settlers in Pennsylvania brought the custom of an Easter-egg tree to America.

A very old and popular Easter game is an egg-rolling contest. Boys and girls roll hard-boiled eggs down a grassy slope. When the eggs hit against each other, they usually crack. The winner is the boy or girl whose egg is the last one to crack.

The most famous egg-rolling contest of all takes place on the lawn of the White House, where the President of the United States lives. The custom started many years ago, under our fourth President, James Madison.

At Easter time boys and girls like to go on an egg hunt. They scurry around to see who can find the most eggs hidden in the house or garden. Sometimes the eggs are real eggs. Sometimes they are brightly colored candy ones.

The Easter rabbit is supposed to bring the Easter eggs and hide them. He is very shy. He comes at night, and no one ever sees him.

No one knows how the story of the Easter rabbit began. But the rabbit is an old, old symbol of the spring festival. It stands for the abundance of new life.

Many Easter customs have come down
to us from long ago. Often they have
changed along the way.

In the days of the early Christians,
Easter was the time when new members
of the church were baptized. Afterward
they put on new white clothes as a sign of
their joy. Now everyone likes to wear
something new on Easter Sunday.

In Europe many people still carry on the old custom of taking a walk after church on Easter. They like to walk through the fields to see the flowers and listen to the birds.

In New York City this old Easter custom has turned into a fashion parade on Fifth Avenue.

On Easter Sunday millions of Christians attend outdoor services, often on a hill where they can see the sun rise. There is an old saying that the sun dances as it rises on Easter morning.

Inside the churches Easter lilies bloom before the altars. Organ music peals forth. People lift up their voices and sing.

All Christian churches do not celebrate the Easter season in the same way. But the message of Easter is always the same. It is the message of life without end. It is the good news of what happened to Jesus of Nazareth more than nineteen hundred years ago.

Everyone knows something about the life of Jesus.

As a boy he lived in the small town of
Nazareth near the Sea of Galilee. When
he was about thirty years old, he began
teaching and preaching, and healing the
sick. His fame spread quickly.

Soon he had twelve disciples, or fol-
lowers. Most of them were fishermen. They
went with Jesus and learned from him as
he walked through the countryside talking
to the people.

Crowds gathered to hear Jesus preach. They found new hope and strength in the words he spoke. Many people began to say that he was the king, or Messiah, they had long been waiting for.

Early one spring Jesus and his disciples walked the long rough road to Jerusalem to celebrate the Passover, the spring festival of the Jews. Bright windflowers, which Jesus called lilies of the field, bloomed along the way.

On a mild Sunday morning Jesus rode into Jerusalem on a donkey. People cheered and waved branches of palm trees to welcome him. They spread palm branches before him. They cried: "Blessed is the King of Israel that cometh in the name of the Lord."

In honor of this day Christian churches all over the world now celebrate Palm Sunday, the first day of Holy Week. Often palm branches or little crosses made of palm leaves are given out at the end of the service.

After that first Palm Sunday, Jesus preached in the outer halls of the great temple at Jerusalem for several days. People crowded around to listen and to praise him.

But he had enemies, too. Priests and other strict Jews accused Jesus of breaking the laws of their religion. Besides, they were afraid he was getting too much power over the people.

On Thursday evening Jesus ate the Passover supper in Jerusalem with his twelve disciples. During the meal he rose from the table. He took a basin of water and began to wash the feet of his disciples.

When he finished, he said, "I have given you an example, that ye should do as I have done to you." Then he gave his disciples a new commandment. "Love one another even as I have loved you," he said.

We now call this meal the Last Supper. It came on the evening of the day we call Maundy Thursday.

For many years the chief ceremony on Maundy Thursday was washing the feet of poor men, to show friendship and humbleness. Nowadays people give Maundy money to the needy instead.

After washing the feet of his disciples, Jesus talked to them for a long time. Then he led them to a large garden outside the walls of Jerusalem to spend the night. He did this even though he knew that Judas, one of the twelve, would tell his enemies where to find him.

Toward morning, Judas led a band of temple guards to the garden. They seized Jesus. The other disciples were so afraid they ran away.

The council of priests found Jesus guilty of speaking against the things the priests held sacred. They wanted him put to death. But first they had to take him to the Roman governor, Pontius Pilate. "He stirreth up the people," they charged. "We found this fellow saying that he himself is Christ a King."

At first Pilate found no fault in Jesus. He asked, "What will ye then that I shall do unto him whom ye call King of the Jews?"

The enemies of Jesus shouted, "Crucify him! Crucify him!"

"Shall I crucify your King?" asked Pilate.

"We have no king but Caesar," shouted the chief priests.

Then Pilate handed Jesus over to the priests.

Soldiers took him to a hill outside Jerusalem and nailed him to a cross, like a common thief.

This happened on Friday morning, a day we now call Good Friday, or God's Friday. For Christians it is a day of sadness. Many churches hold a three-hour service, beginning at noon. Short sermons about the last words Jesus spoke from the cross are part of the service.

Before the sun went down on that first Good Friday in Jerusalem, friends of Jesus took his lifeless body from the cross. They laid it in a stone tomb and rolled a great stone before the door.

At sunrise Sunday morning, Mary Magdalene and two other women went to the tomb. The big stone was rolled away!

They looked into the tomb and saw a young man dressed in a white robe. "Do not be amazed," he said to them. "Ye seek Jesus of Nazareth, which was crucified. He is risen; he is not here."

The women ran to tell the news to the disciples. They did not know what to think. Then they remembered. While they were still in Galilee, Jesus had told them that he would be crucified. And he had also told them, "After three days I will rise again." This was the third day.

On that first Easter Sunday Jesus appeared to the disciples and to other people. He spoke to them. He walked with them. He told the disciples to go back to Galilee.

His disciples went back to their fishing
boats. They felt like lost sheep without
their shepherd.

One night they fished all night and
caught nothing. As they rowed to shore at
sunrise, they saw a man on the beach. He
called to them. He told them to throw
their net on the right side of the boat. They
did, and caught so many fish they could
hardly pull in the net.

The man on the shore was Jesus. He said to his disciples, "Feed my lambs. Tend my sheep. Go into all the world and preach the good news."

Now the disciples knew what Jesus wanted them to do. They were no longer afraid. They would go "into all the world" and spread the good news of the risen Christ and his teachings.

That is what the disciples did. And that is how the Christian church was started.

The miracle of Jesus' rising from death to new life is the great message of Easter.

No wonder it is a day of rejoicing.

ABOUT THE AUTHOR

Aileen Fisher lives in a cabin on a ranch in the foothills of Colorado—a cabin which she helped build with her own hands. From the window by her desk she looks beyond fields and pine-covered hills to Arapahoe Glacier.

Born in the Upper Peninsula of Michigan, Miss Fisher spent her childhood in the country. Her love of the outdoors has continued to be an important influence in her life. During high school years she wrote her first poetry for the school column in the local paper. Since graduation from college she has written many books for children, among them *Fisherman of Galilee*, the story of Simon Peter and the ministry of Jesus. She has also written *And Yet Have Believed*, an Easter cantata.

ABOUT THE ILLUSTRATOR

Some of the Easter eggs that appear in this book may well be replicas of those hanging on a tree at the Forbergs' home in Brooklyn, New York. Over the years, Ati Forberg and her husband and children have been painting elaborate Easter eggs for their sizable collection.

Mrs. Forberg is a native of Germany. She came to live in the United States after a stay in England and studied here at Black Mountain College in Black Mountain, North Carolina. She has been involved in many phases of graphic design including book jackets and advertising, exhibits, and window display.

EASTER